EVERYBODY'S STRUM & PLAY GUITAR CHORDS

Learn the Art of Strumming and Fingerpicking Chords with this Step-by-Step Approach

Philip Groeber
David Hoge
Rey Sanchez

FREE Downloadable Recordings!

Production: Frank J. Hackinson
Production Coordinator: Philip Groeber
Cover: Terpstra Design, San Francisco
Text Editor: Pamela Hoge
Engraving: Tempo Music Press, Inc.
Printer: Tempo Music Press, Inc.

THE
F·J·H
MUSIC
COMPANY
INC.
Frank J. Hackinson

ISBN-13: 978-1-56939-733-6

T0019053

Contents

G1042

Alphabetical Song Titles

Note: The pieces in this book are composed by the authors unless otherwise indicated.

HOLDING THE GUITAR

Sitting

The guitar should rest comfortably on your lap. The right leg may be crossed over the left leg for added support.

Standing

A guitar strap is used to hold the guitar in correct playing position. A strap may also be used in the sitting position.

Classical position

The left leg is raised by a footstand, which places the guitar in a very secure position.

The Left Hand

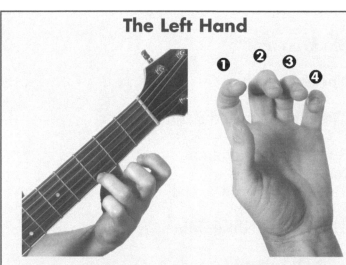

- The left-hand fingers are numbered 1, 2, 3, and 4 as shown.

- Press with the fingertip directly behind the fret. Use just enough pressure to produce a clear sound. For best results, the left-hand fingernails should be kept short.

- The thumb should touch lightly on the back of the guitar neck opposite the finger tips. It remains in a natural position. The palm does not touch the back of the neck.

The Right Hand

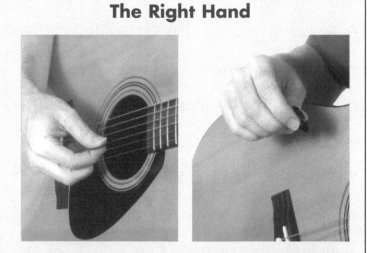

- The **pick** (flat-pick or plectrum) is used to strum the strings.

- Some students may choose to use the right-hand thumb and fingers instead of a pick.

- If using a pick, start with a teardrop shape of medium thickness.

- Hold the pick in a relaxed, secure way.

- The strings may be sounded by using **downstrokes** (⊓) or **upstrokes** (∨) with the guitar pick.

G1042

TUNING THE GUITAR

It is very important that your guitar be tuned correctly each time you practice.

 Tuning Notes: E B G D A E

1. Electronic tuner

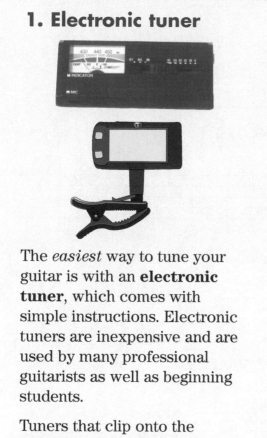

The *easiest* way to tune your guitar is with an **electronic tuner**, which comes with simple instructions. Electronic tuners are inexpensive and are used by many professional guitarists as well as beginning students.

Tuners that clip onto the headstock make tuning the guitar a little easier.

2. Piano keyboard

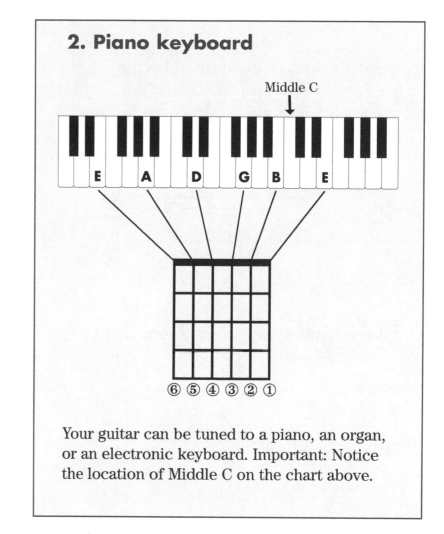

Your guitar can be tuned to a piano, an organ, or an electronic keyboard. Important: Notice the location of Middle C on the chart above.

3. Tuning the guitar to itself (relative tuning)

Assuming that string ⑥ is correctly tuned to **E**:			
PRESS	**STRING**	**TO GET THE PITCH**	**TO TUNE OPEN STRING**
the 5th fret of	⑥	**A**	⑤
the 5th fret of	⑤	**D**	④
the 5th fret of	④	**G**	③
the 4th fret of	③	**B**	②
the 5th fret of	②	**E**	①

MUSIC FUNDAMENTALS

THE STAFF

Music is written on the **staff**, which has five lines and four spaces.

THE TREBLE CLEF

The **treble** (or **G**) **clef** is placed at the beginning (left side) of each staff of guitar music.

LINE NOTES

Each **line** has a letter name:

Every **G**uitar **B**eginner **D**oes **F**ine

SPACE NOTES

Each **space** has a letter name:

F A C E

PITCH

Pitch is the highness or lowness of a music tone. The higher the pitch, the higher a note is placed on the staff. The lower the pitch, the lower a note is placed on the staff. The names of notes come from the music alphabet A–G.

RHYTHM VALUES

notes strums rests

		whole	= 4 beats
		dotted half	= 3 beats
		half	= 2 beats
		quarter	= 1 beat
		eighth	= ½ beat

Note values (o ♩. ♩ ♩ ♪) indicate the duration of each pitch. Each musical note indicates both the pitch to be played *and* how long to let the tone sound.

BAR LINES AND MEASURES

Bar lines divide the staff into equal parts called **measures**. An **ending bar line** is used to show the end of a piece of music.

THE TIME SIGNATURE

The 4/4 (four-four) **time signature** tells us:

4 = four beats per measure

4 = the quarter note (♩) gets one beat

Count: 1   2   3   4

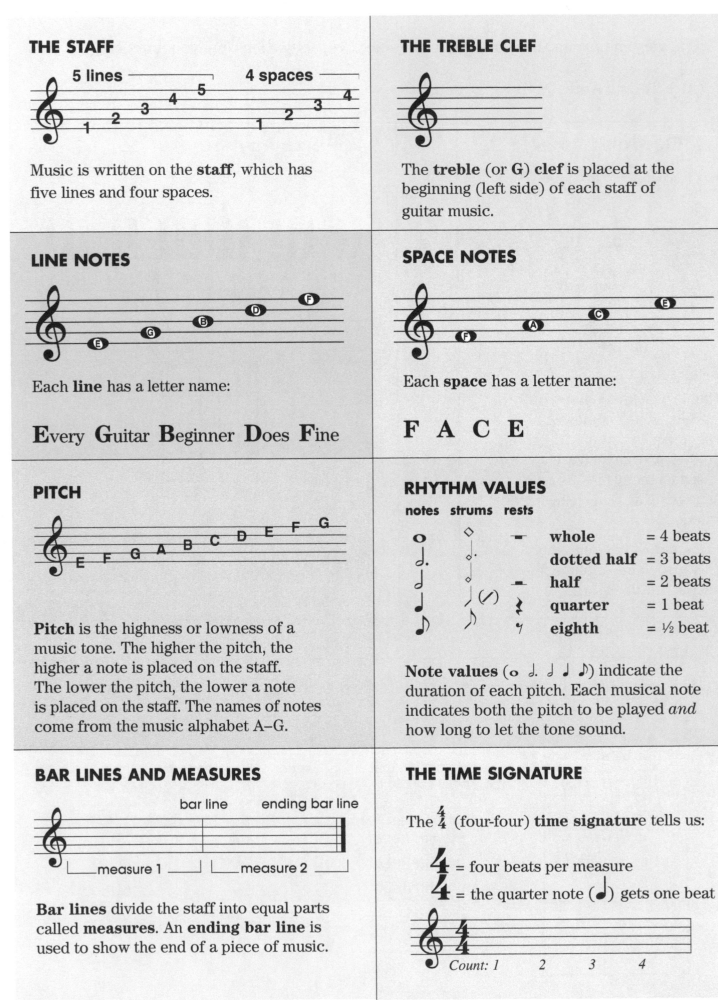

G1042

GETTING STARTED

- A **chord** consists of two or more notes played at the same time. Most chords on the guitar use four, five, or six strings.

- In this book, each new chord will be introduced on a fingerboard diagram. A photograph will often be included to show correct left-hand form.

- Use the following example as a guide to learn the new chords presented in this book.

Fingerboard Diagram

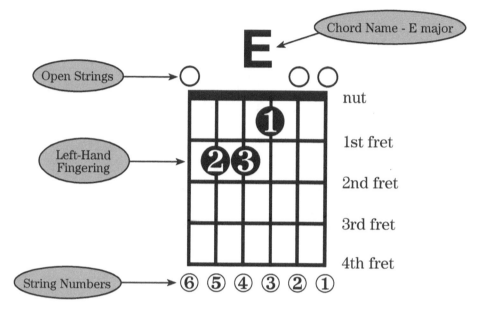

- Chord names and strum marks (∕) will usually be shown above the staff.

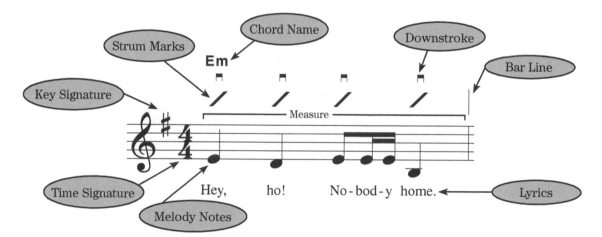

CHORD BASICS
(THREE-STRING CHORDS)

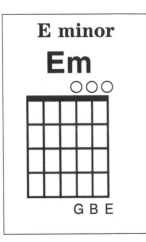

E minor
Em

G B E

To play Em, simply play the open third, second, and first strings.

Although this version of Em uses no left-hand fingers, keep your left hand in a ready-to-play position.

Use a **downstroke** (⊓) to play Em: allow the pick (or thumb) to glide smoothly across the first three strings.

BASIC STRUM

- The **basic strum** is a downstroke (⊓) on each beat of every measure. Chord strums will be written out in slash notation (╱ = **quarter note strum**).

- Songs with the time signature of $\frac{4}{4}$ usually get four equal strums (beats) per measure.

- Strum marks may sometimes be placed inside the staff as below.

③ Hey, Ho, Nobody Home

Traditional English Round

Capo the 5th fret for singing. Key of Am

♩ = 60   Hey,   ho!   No - bod - y   home.   Food   nor   drink   nor   mon - ey   have   I   none.

Repeat as needed

Yet   will   I   be   mer   -   ry.   Hey,   ho!   No - bod - y   home.

Repeat Sign

* As the first soloist/singer starts measure two, the second soloist/singer starts to play measure one.

G1042

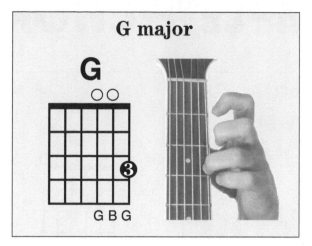

- Remember to strum chords softly and evenly on every beat, even if the melody has a different rhythm.

④ *Frère Jacques*
(Are You Sleeping?)

Traditional French Round

Frè - re   Jac - ques,   Frè - re   Jac - ques,   dor - mez-vous?   Dor - mez-vous?
Are   you   sleep - ing?   Are   you   sleep - ing?   Broth - er   John,   Broth - er   John,

Son - nez   les   ma - ti - nes,   son - nez   les   ma - tin - es;   Din,   dan,   don!   Din,   dan,   don!
Morn - ing   bells   are   ring - ing,   morn - ing   bells   are   ring - ing;   Ding,   dong,   ding!   Ding,   dong,   ding!

Strum with a steady beat. The pulse of music is just as important as playing the correct notes or chords. Think of your right hand as being the drummer in a band, whose job is to keep the rhythm even and consistent.

A **round** is a song in which the lyrics can be repeated over and over, with the performers starting at different times. Player two begins at measure one when player one begins the measure marked with an asterisk (*).

COMPLETE CHORDS

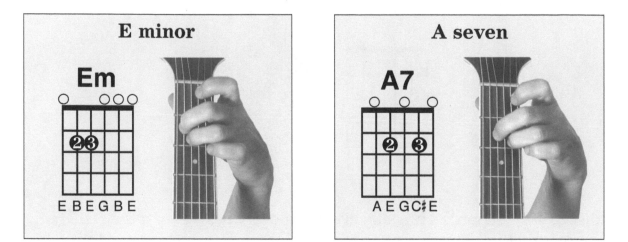

CHANGING CHORDS

- Memorize the location of the left-hand fingers for each new chord. Notice that Em and A7 have similar left-hand shapes.
- When changing from one chord to the next, move your left hand (and fingers) quickly so your right hand can strum with a steady beat (without stopping or hesitating).
- Practice the following example several times without stopping the pulse of the music. Count out loud as you strum evenly.

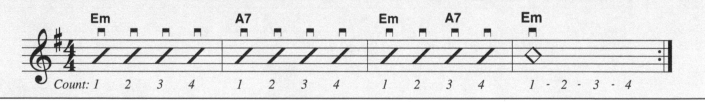

 Complete chords include four, five, or six strings. If a string is not played open or is not played by the left hand, do not strum the string with your right hand. Therefore, A7 is a five-string chord.

⑤ Two-Chord Blues

G1042

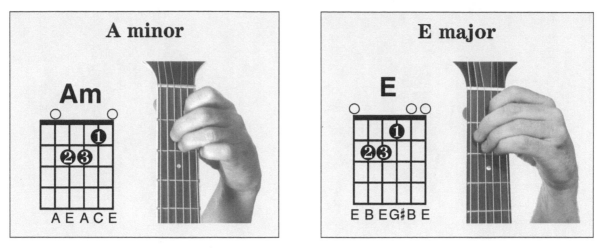

A minor — Am — A E A C E

E major — E — E B E G♯ B E

- Songs with the time signature of ¾ get three strums per measure. Strum with a steady beat!

| Am | | | E | | | | | | Am | dotted half-note strum (3 beats) |

Count: 1   2   3   1   2   3   1   2   3   1 - 2 - 3

⑥ Latvian Lullaby

Latvian Folksong

Am

♩ = 112

Lull - a - by, my ba - by,_____ soft - ly

E

sleeps the child._____ Sis - ter rocks you

Am   E   Am

gent - ly,_____ she is soft and mild._____

chord chops

The E chord is one of the best sounding chords on the guitar. The following chord progression is based on the E chord shape, moved one fret higher. The chord names F and G only approximate the harmony. Be sure to memorize this popular progression.

⑦ Spanish Bullfight

E   F   G   F   E

♩ = 92

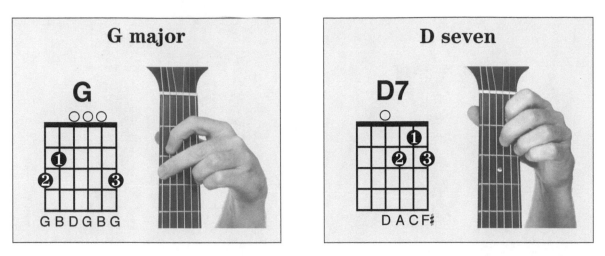

- Strum with a steady beat! Be sure to allow all strums held for two beats or longer to ring out for their full value.

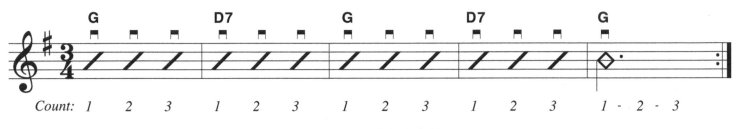

Count: 1   2   3   1   2   3   1   2   3   1   2   3   1 - 2 - 3

PICK-UP NOTES

Pick-up notes are notes that come before the first complete measure. The beats in the pick-up measure and the last measure usually add up to one full measure. *Begin strumming in the first complete measure.*

⑧ The More We Get Together

Traditional American

Capo the 5th fret for singing. Key of C

G1042

Hush Little Baby

Carolina Folksong

1. Hush, lit-tle ba-by don't say a word; Pa-pa's gon-na buy you a mock-ing-bird.

If that mock-ing - bird don't sing, Pa-pa's gon-na buy you a dia-mond ring.

2. If that __ dia-mond ring turns __ brass, Pa-pa's gon-na buy you a look-ing glass.

If that look-ing glass gets broke, Pa-pa's gon-na buy you a bil-ly goat.

Additional Lyrics

3. And if that billy goat won't pull,
   Papa's gonna buy you a cart and bull.
   And if that cart and bull turn over,
   Papa's gonna buy you a dog named Rover.

4. And if that dog named Rover won't bark,
   Papa's gonna buy you a horse and cart.
   And if that horse and cart fall down,
   You'll still be the sweetest little baby in town.

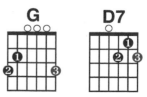

Guide fingers *are fingers that keep gentle contact with the strings when changing between chords. For example, keep your third finger on the first string when changing from G to D7 or D7 to G.*

Endings *are very important when strumming chord accompaniment. If you are ever in doubt about how to end a song, strum one extra chord at the very end of the song and let it ring out. Always have a definite ending.*

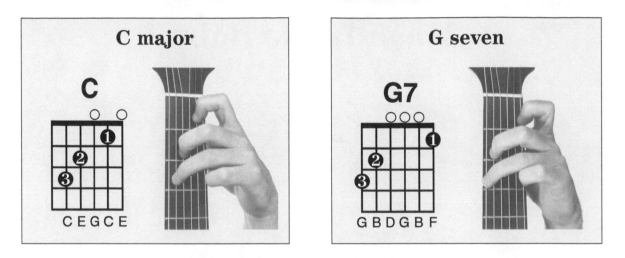

C major — C — C E G C E

G seven — G7 — G B D G B F

- Notice that C and G7 have similar left-hand shapes. Strum with a steady beat!

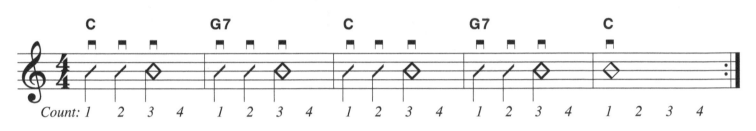

Count: 1 2 3 4 1 2 3 4 1 2 3 4 1 2 3 4 1 2 3 4

⑩ Skip to My Lou

Traditional Folksong

Capo the 5th fret for singing. Key of F

♩ = 104   Flies in the but-ter-milk, shoo, fly, shoo! Flies in the but-ter-milk, shoo, fly, shoo!

Flies in the but-ter-milk, shoo, fly, shoo! Skip to my Lou, my dar - ling!

Skip, skip, skip to my Lou, skip, skip, skip to my Lou,

Skip, skip, skip to my Lou, skip to my Lou, my dar - ling!

G1042

Dynamics are symbols and words that indicate how loud or soft to play.
The following symbols are used in this book:

p = *piano* (soft) mf = *mezzo forte* (medium loud) f = *forte* (loud)

If the music has no dynamic level indicated, play mf (medium loud).

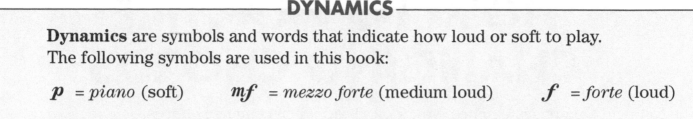

⑪ *Sur le pont d'Avignon*

Traditional French Folksong

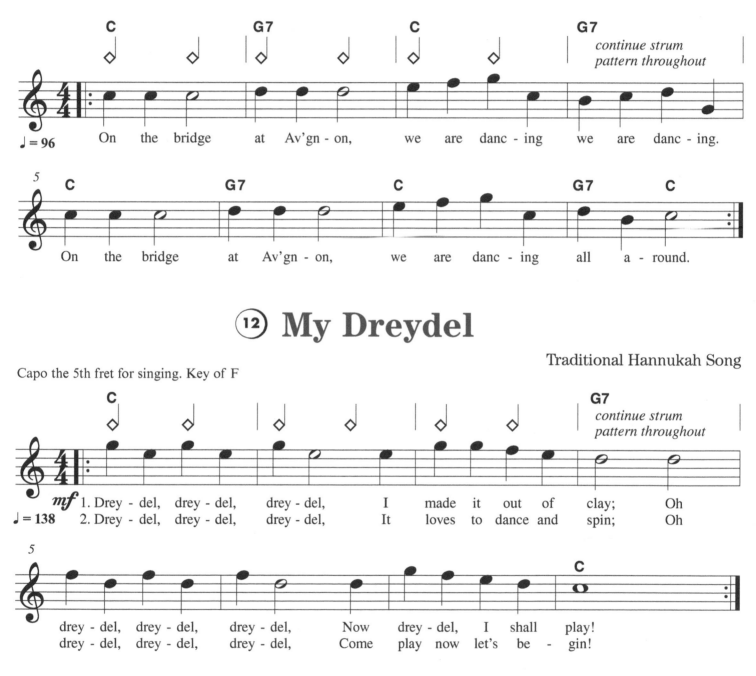

Capo the 5th fret for singing. Key of F

continue strum pattern throughout

♩ = 96

On the bridge at Av'gn - on, we are danc - ing we are danc - ing.

On the bridge at Av'gn - on, we are danc - ing all a - round.

⑫ **My Dreydel**

Traditional Hannukah Song

Capo the 5th fret for singing. Key of F

continue strum pattern throughout

mf ♩ = 138

1. Drey - del, drey - del, drey - del, I made it out of clay; Oh
2. Drey - del, drey - del, drey - del, It loves to dance and spin; Oh

drey - del, drey - del, drey - del, Now drey - del, I shall play!
drey - del, drey - del, drey - del, Come play now let's be - gin!

When strumming chords, the accompanist for a vocalist or soloist must be sure that the melody can be heard at all times. Adjust your volume as needed.

HOW TO PRACTICE CHANGING CHORDS

The following exercises can help you look ahead when changing chords.

- Strum (╱) four times on Em, four times on all open strings, four times on A7, and four more times on all open strings.

- While strumming the open strings, look ahead to the next chord shape. Be sure to keep a steady beat. An even rhythm is very important while strumming chords.

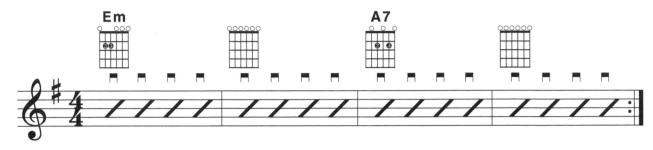

- Once you can play the above exercise without pausing, strum the open strings for only two beats.

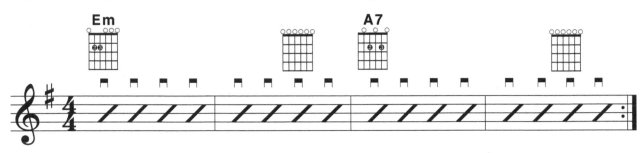

- Now strum the open strings for only one beat.

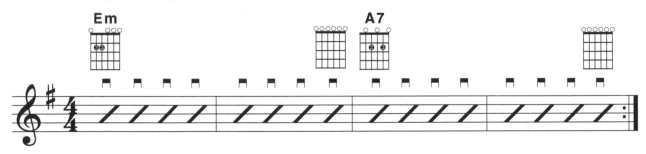

- As you play the following example, you should now be able to visualize the chord changes very easily.

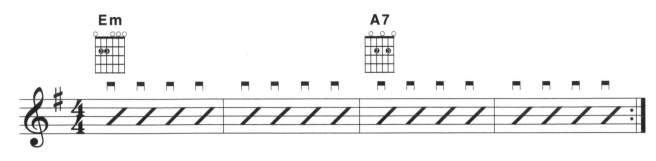

 **test yourself** **Use the above chord changing techniques on other chord combinations you have learned.   Am - E   G - D7   C - G7**
Use these techniques when learning any new chords.

G1042

Common fingers are fingers that remain in position when changing chords. For example, keep your first finger in the same place for both the C and D7 chords.

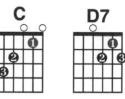

C **D7**

(13) # This Old Man

Traditional American Folksong

Capo the 5th fret for singing. Key of C

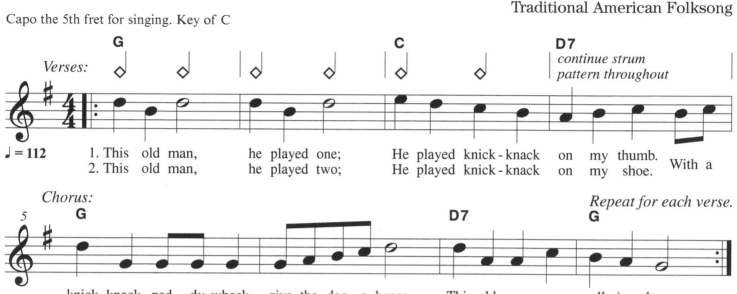

♩ = 112

1. This old man, he played one; He played knick-knack on my thumb. With a
2. This old man, he played two; He played knick-knack on my shoe. With a

Chorus: *Repeat for each verse.*

knick-knack, pad-dy whack, give the dog a bone; This old man came roll-ing home.

Additional Lyrics

3. This old man, he played three;
   He played knick-knack on my knee. *Chorus:*
4. This old man, he played four;
   He played knick-knack on my door. *Chorus:*
5. This old man, he played five;
   He played knick-knack on my hive. *Chorus:*
6. This old man, he played six;
   He played knick-knack on my sticks. *Chorus:*

7. This old man, he played seven;
   He played knick-knack up in heaven. *Chorus:*
8. This old man, he played eight;
   He played knick-knack on my gate. *Chorus:*
9. This old man, he played nine;
   He played knick-knack on my spine. *Chorus:*
10. This old man, he played ten;
   He played knick-knack once again. *Chorus:*

(14) # If You're Happy and You Know It

Traditional

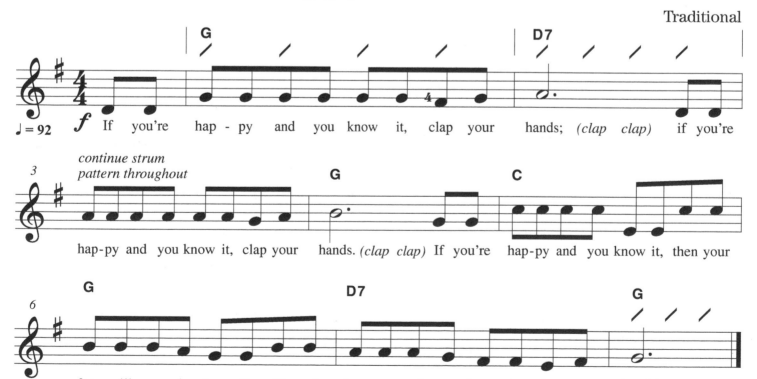

♩ = 92 *f*

If you're hap-py and you know it, clap your hands; *(clap clap)* if you're

hap-py and you know it, clap your hands. *(clap clap)* If you're hap-py and you know it, then your

face will sure-ly show it; if you're hap-py and you know it, clap your hands! *(clap clap)*

G1042

15 She'll Be Comin' 'Round the Mountain

Traditional

continue strum pattern throughout

♩ = 112 𝆑 She'll be com-in' 'round the moun-tain when she comes._____ She'll be

com-in' 'round the moun-tain when she comes._____ She'll be

com-in' 'round the moun-tain, she'll be com-in' 'round the

moun-tain, she'll be com-in' 'round the moun-tain when she comes._____

16 Happy Birthday to You

Words by Mildred J. Hill and Patty S. Hill
Music Traditional

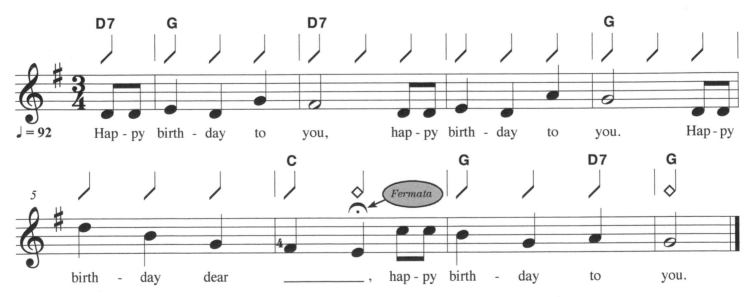

♩ = 92 Hap-py birth-day to you, hap-py birth-day to you. Hap-py

Fermata

birth-day dear _____, hap-py birth-day to you.

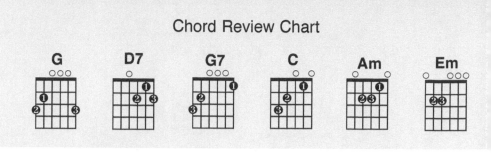

⑰ Simple Gifts

Traditional

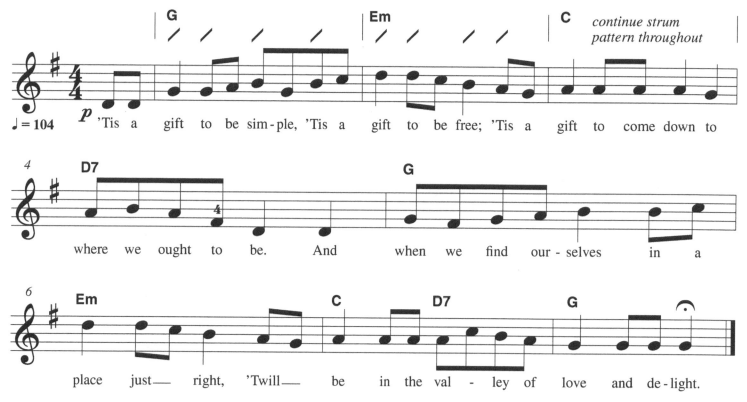

♩ = 104   *p* 'Tis a gift to be sim-ple, 'Tis a gift to be free; 'Tis a gift to come down to

where we ought to be. And when we find our-selves in a

place just— right, 'Twill— be in the val - ley of love and de-light.

When strumming chords, the accompanist must be sure to provide a steady beat for the soloist. Do not strum the same rhythm as the melody. Remember you are also functioning as the drummer, providing a steady pulse.

Sometimes moving chord shapes around on the guitar fingerboard creates new and unusual sounds. This makes it difficult to come up with accurate chord names.

Chord With No Name uses a chord very similar to Em, but moves the fingers to different strings on the same fret. Maybe you can invent some of your own chord shapes!

⑱ Chord With No Name

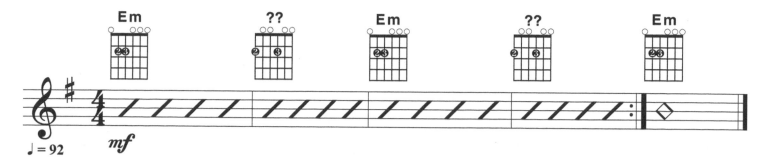

Em   ??   Em   ??   Em

♩ = 92   *mf*

G1042

19

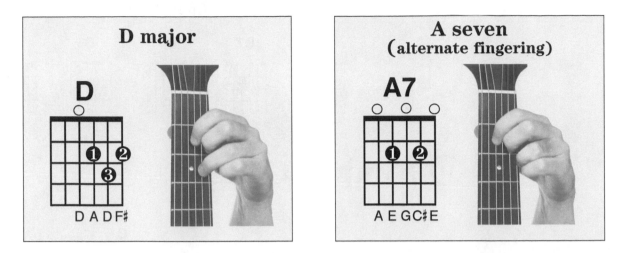

D major

A seven
(alternate fingering)

- Always strum with a steady pulse! Be sure to strum only four strings when playing the D chord.

⑲ He's Got the Whole World in His Hands

Traditional

Capo the 2nd fret for singing. Key of E

1. He's got the whole world—— in His hands;— He's got the whole wide world—— in His hands;— He's got the whole world—— in His hands;—— He's got the whole world in His hands.

♩ = 96

Additional Lyrics

2. He's got my brothers and my sisters in His hands;
   He's got my brothers and my sisters in His hands;
   He's got my brothers and my sisters in His hands;
   He's got the whole world in His hands.

3. He's got the sun and the rain in His hands;
   He's got the moon and the stars in His hands;
   He's got the wind and the clouds in His hands;
   He's got the whole world in His hands.

4. He's got the rivers and the mountains in His hands;
   He's got the oceans and the seas in His hands;
   He's got you and he's got me in His hands;
   He's got the whole world in His hands.

5. He's got everybody here in His hands;
   He's got everybody there in His hands;
   He's got everybody everywhere in His hands;
   He's got the whole world in His hands.

G1042

When the Saints Go Marching In

Traditional American

Capo the 2nd fret for singing. Key of E

continue strum pattern throughout

♩ = 132

1. Oh, when the saints,————— go march-ing in,————— oh, when the
2. And when the sun,————— re - fuse to shine,————— and when the

saints go march - ing in,————— Oh, I
sun re - fuse to shine.————— Oh, I

want to be in that num - ber,————— when the
want to be in that num - ber,————— when the

saints go march - ing in.—————
sun re - fuse to shine.—————

Always keep your right hand moving with a steady pulse when strumming chords.

The following chord progression is a favorite among guitarists. Be sure that the 1st string E sounds clearly in the D(add9) chord.

㉑ Sounds Good!

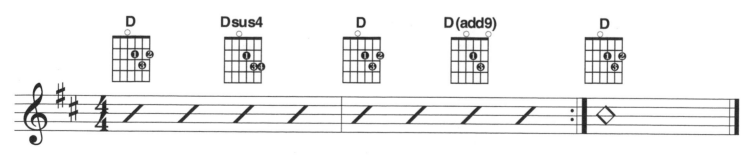

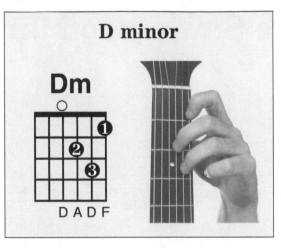

D minor

Dm

D A D F

• Strum with a steady beat!

㉒ The Snake Charmer

Traditional

continue strum pattern throughout

♩ = 152   *f*

test yourself

Memorize the three types of D chords below. Say the chord names out loud as you switch from one chord to the next. Be able to change quickly between these chords while maintaining a clear sound.

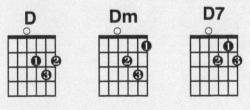

D   **Dm**   **D7**

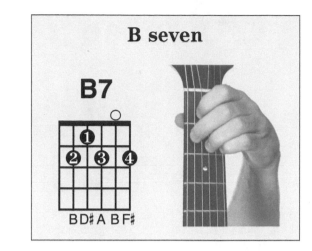

B seven

B7

BD#A B F#

㉓ Here Is the Cradle

Norwegian Lullaby

Em   B7   Em   B7

continue strum pattern throughout

1. Here is the cra - dle pre - pared for your sleep,
2. An - gels shall come soon, their vig - il to keep,

safe and so warm, lit - tle ba - by.
watch o - ver you, lit - tle ba - by.

Loo, loo, now go to sleep, so

sweet - ly to sleep, lit - tle ba - by.

chord chops

Have fun playing these great sounding chords. Notice the variation of the G chord.

㉔ Campfire Chords

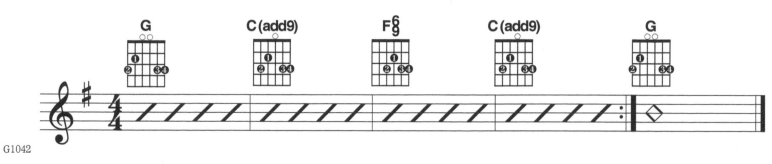

G   C(add9)   F⁶₉   C(add9)   G

(25) Aura Lee

Traditional

1. As the black-bird in the spring, 'neath the wil-low tree,
2. Take my heart and take my ring, I give my all to thee,

sat and piped, I heard him sing, sing of Au-ra Lee!
take me for e-ter-ni-ty, dear-est Au-ra Lee!

Chorus:

Au-ra Lee, Au-ra Lee, maid with gold-en hair,

sun-shine came a-long with thee, and swal-lows in the air.

Additional Lyrics

3. In her blush the rose was born, 'twas music when she spoke,
   in her eyes the light of morn, sparkling seemed to break.

4. Aura Lee the bird may flee, the willow's golden hair,
   then the wintry winds may be, blowing ev'rywhere.

Aura Lee is an American Civil War song. Elvis Presley recorded the 1956 song *Love Me Tender* using the same melody as *Aura Lee*.

G1042

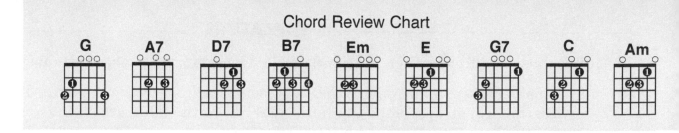

(26) Amazing Grace

Early American

 Make sure to count correctly on the repeats. Do not lose or add any beats.

Guitar music is often written in **tablature** (**TAB**), a centuries-old notation system.

- Tablature is a graphic design that represents each string of the guitar. The 1st string E (the thinnest string) is the top horizontal line of the tablature staff; the sixth string E (the thickest string) is the bottom line.

- The numbers placed on the string indicate which fret is to be played. Numbers placed next to the note heads in the staff indicate left-hand fingering.

- The use of tablature can make guitar music easier to understand. Generally, there are no rhythms indicated in tablature.

(27) Rock Riff

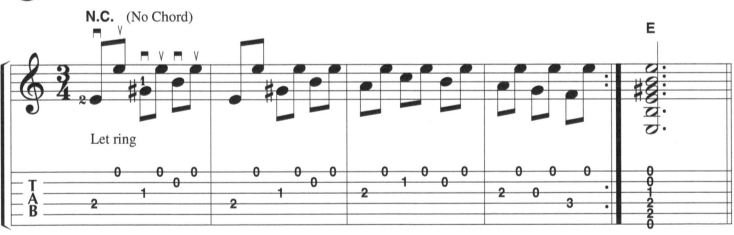

- The use of tablature makes it easier to read music that looks difficult, as in *Malagueña*.

(27) *Malagueña*

- The first measure in *Blues Ending* uses a descending D7 chord shape.

(27) Blues Ending

26

G1042

Play the first ending and take the repeat.
Then play the second ending, skipping over the first ending.

(28) Bingo

* On each repeat, the singers substitute a hand clap for each letter in the spelling of the name *Bingo*.

chord chops

The following progression uses a movable Dm chord shape. See page 50 for more information on slash chords (Em/D, F/D).

(29) Keep the Change

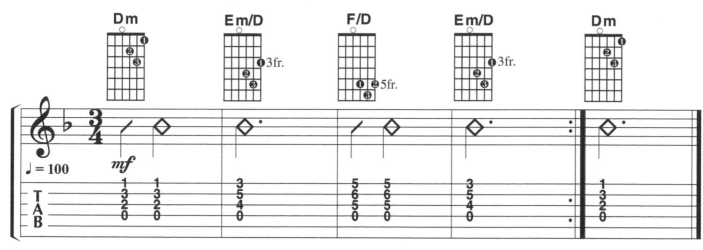

The **root strum** is a very popular technique that makes it sound as if two people are playing at the same time!

- When playing in $\frac{4}{4}$ time, use a downstroke to play the lowest-pitched **root note** (**R**) of the chord on beat one.

- Strum strings ③, ②, and ① on beats two, three and four. Be sure your left hand plays *all* of the notes in the chord, not only the notes indicated in the tablature.

- The root note (**R**) should continue to sound as you strum the rest of the chord. Practice the following root strum example using the D chord.

㉚ Mary Ann

Traditional Caribbean

Capo the 2nd fret for singing. Key of E

G1042

(31) Molly Malone

Traditional Irish Melody

= 120

1. In Dub - lin's fair cit - y where the girls are so pret - ty, 'twas

there I first met with sweet Mol - ly Ma - lone. She

drove a wheel - bar - row through streets broad and nar - row, sing - ing

"Cock - les and mus - sels, a - live all a - live."

Additional Lyrics

2. Now she was a fishmonger,
   And sure 'twas no wonder,
   For so were her mother and father before,
   And they each wheeled their barrow,
   Through streets broad and narrow,
   Crying, "Cockles and mussels, alive, all alive!"

3. She died of a fever,
   And no one could save her,
   And that was the end of sweet Molly Malone.
   Now her ghost wheels her barrow,
   Through streets broad and narrow,
   Crying, "Cockles and mussels, alive, all alive!"

A root strum accompaniment in ¾ time is known as a **waltz strum**.

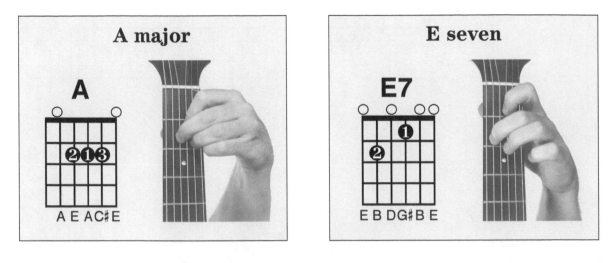

A major

A E AC#E

E seven

E B DG#B E

㉜ Oh! Susanna

Stephen Foster

Capo the 5th fret for singing. Key of E

continue strum pattern throughout

♩ = 120

f 1. I come from Al - a - bam - a with a ban - jo on my knee; I'm
rained all night the day I left, the weath - er it was dry; The

goin' to Lou - 'si - an - a, my— true love for to see. 2. It cry.
sun so hot I froze to death, Su - san - na don't you

Chorus:
Oh! Su - san - na, now don't you cry for me; I

come from Al - a - bam - a with a ban - jo on my knee.

Stephen Foster (1826-1864) is one of the most famous American composers. Some of his most popular songs are: *Beautiful Dreamer, Camptown Races, My Old Kentucky Home, Old Folks at Home,* and *Some Folks Do.*

G1042

(33) *A la nanita nana*

Traditional Spanish Carol

Capo the 5th fret for singing. Key of Dm

A quarter-note strum may be divided into two equal parts called **eighth-note strums**.
A single eighth-note strum has a flag (♪). Two or more eighth-note strums may be connected by a beam (♫).

♪ = ½ beat   ♫ = 1 beat   = 2 beats

Practice the following eighth-note strum on various chords using downstrokes and upstrokes.
When using upstrokes, it is only necessary to strum two or three strings, *not* all six.

③④ Sailor Song

Sea Chantey

Capo the 5th fret for singing. Key of Am

♩ = 112

1. What do you do with a wea - ry sail - or,
2. Put him in his bed wait un - til he wakes up,

what do you do with a wea - ry sail - or?
put him in his bed wait un - til he wakes up.

What do you do with a wea - ry sail - or,
Put him in his bed wait un - til he wakes up,

ear - ly in the morn - ing?
ear - ly in the morn - ing!

32

(35) Sloop John B.

Traditional Caribbean

continue strum pattern throughout

♩ = 112

We come on the Sloop John B. my grand-fath-er and me. A-round Nas-sau Town we-did roam.___ Play-in' all night.___ We got in-to a fight.___ I feel so break___ up, I wan-na go home.___

Experiment using different strums other than the one indicated. Be consistent, using the same strum pattern throughout a song. However, get comfortable with many different strums so that your accompaniment styles will be varied.

Use all downstrokes to play the eighth-note strums in this popular chord progression.

(36) Born to Strum

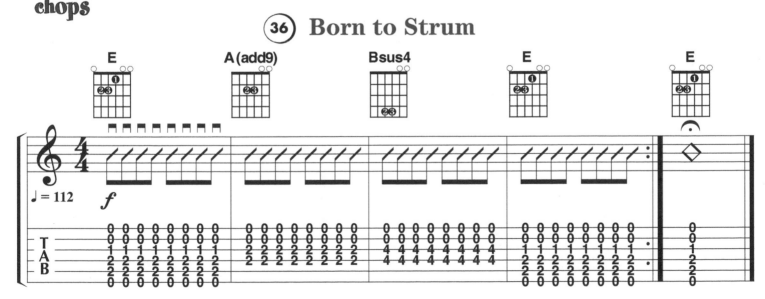

♩ = 112 *f*

ROOT AND FIFTH STRUM

Another bass note to add to the root strum is the **fifth** of the chord. You can quickly find the name of the fifth by counting on your fingers. The fifth may be a higher pitch or a lower pitch than the root.

- Below is a chart of the roots (R) and fifths (5) for many of the major, minor, and seventh chords.

- Memorize the locations of all roots and fifths. Play R / 5 / on all chords to get familiar with this strum.

- Notice that it is necessary to move a left-hand finger in order to play the fifths on the B and C chords. Keep all other fingers in place.

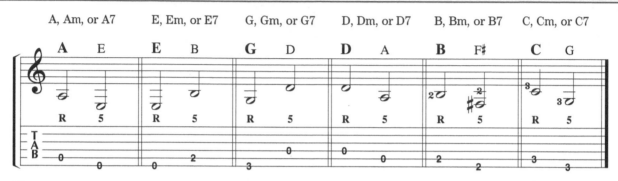

⟨37⟩ Joshua Fit the Battle of Jericho

American Spiritual

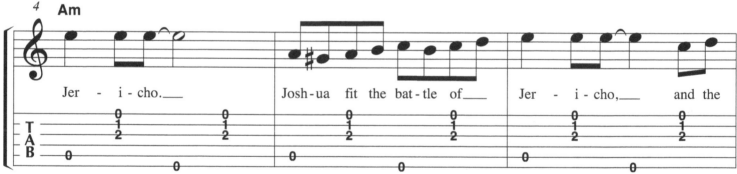

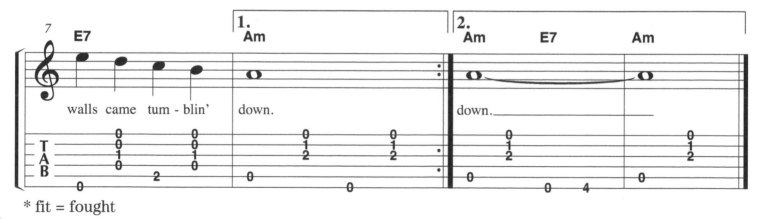

* fit = fought

G1042

38 *Hava Nagila*

Israeli Folksong

New Strum Pattern

Kum Ba Yah
(Come By Here)

African American

Capo the 5th fret for singing. Key of C

♩ = 112

1. Some-one's cry-ing Lord,_____ Kum Ba

continue strum pattern throughout

Yah._____ Some-one's cry-ing Lord,_____ Kum Ba

Yah._____ Some-one's cry-ing Lord,_____ Kum Ba

Yah._____ O Lord,_____ Kum Ba Yah._____

Additional Lyrics

2. Someone's laughing Lord, Kum Ba Yah.
   Someone's laughing Lord, Kum Ba Yah.
   Someone's laughing Lord, Kum Ba Yah.
   O Lord, Kum Ba Yah.

3. Someone's praying Lord, Kum Ba Yah.
   Someone's praying Lord, Kum Ba Yah.
   Someone's praying Lord, Kum Ba Yah.
   O Lord, Kum Ba Yah.

4. Someone's singing Lord, Kum Ba Yah.
   Someone's singing Lord, Kum Ba Yah.
   Someone's singing Lord, Kum Ba Yah.
   O Lord, Kum Ba Yah.

5. Kum Ba Yah, my Lord, Kum Ba Yah.
   Kum Ba Yah, my Lord, Kum Ba Yah.
   Kum Ba Yah, my Lord, Kum Ba Yah.
   O Lord, Kum Ba Yah.

When playing upstrokes (∨), strum three strings or less (not all six!).

G1042

- Now substitute the root note at the beginning of the strum pattern you learned on page 36.

(40) *Arrorró mi niño*
(Lullaby, My Baby)

Argentinean Folksong

continue strum
pattern throughout

♩ = 104

A - rro - rró mi ni - ño,
Lull - a - by, my ba - by,

A - rro - rró mi sol,
Lull - a - by, my son,

A - rro - rró pe -
Lull - a - by, my

da - zo, de mi cor - a - zón.
sweet - heart, Moth - er's lit - tle one.

chord chops

A *barre* chord (pronounced "bar") has one left-hand finger pressing down two or more strings at the same time.

Keeping your first finger just behind the fret will make it easier to get a good sound. Practice the first chord in *Barre-Chord Blues* until all three strings sound clear.

(41) **Barre-Chord Blues**

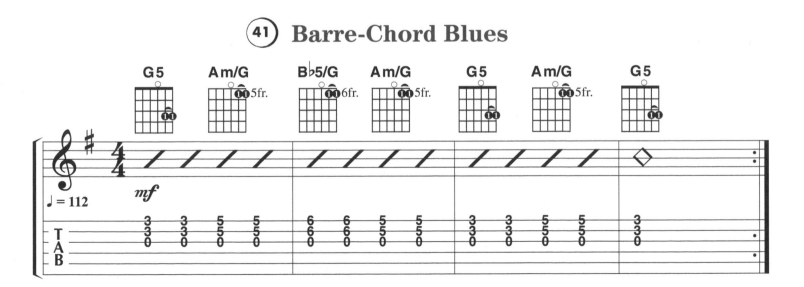

♩ = 112   *mf*

G5   Am/G   B♭5/G   Am/G   G5   Am/G   G5

(42) This Little Light of Mine

American Spiritual

By using an alternate fingering for the G chord (shown below), the transitions between G – G7 and G – C will become much easier.

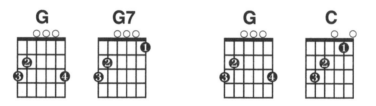

Practice playing roots and fifths on the C and B7 chords before playing "I've Been Working on the Railroad."

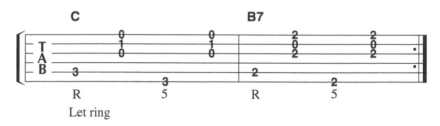

G1042

43 I've Been Working on the Railroad

American Folksong

I've been work-ing on the rail - road, all the live - long day;

I've been work-ing on the rail - road, just to pass the time a - way.

Don't you hear the whis-tle blow - ing, rise up so ear-ly in the morn.

Don't you hear the cap-tain shout - ing, Di - nah blow that horn.

44 The House of the Rising Sun

American Folksong

Capo the 5th fret for singing. Key of Am

♩ = 96

There is a house in New Or - leans, they

call the Ris - ing Sun,_____ and it's been the ru - in of

man - y poor boy, and Lord, I know___ I'm one._____

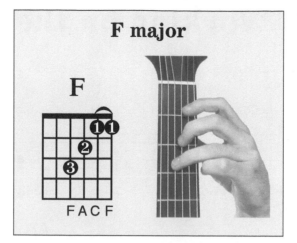

F major

BARRE CHORDS

The F chord uses a *barre* (pronounced "bar") in which one finger holds down two strings.

- First practice the F chord without using the first finger.
  This will help you get your hand and arm into a good position.

- Add the first finger as shown in the photograph above. Notice that you will be pressing somewhat on the side of your first finger. Your left elbow should be slightly tucked in toward your side.

- Practice the F chord *without left-hand pressure* at first. When you press down, keep a relaxed look in your hand and arm.

Learning the F chord can be challenging. Be patient, practicing this chord a little each day. Using barre chords will allow you to play a chord accompaniment to most songs!

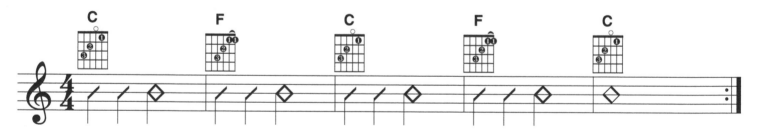

- Because the F chord has no open strings and is **movable**, you may use the F chord shape on higher frets, which makes getting a good sound a little easier.

- Use guide fingers.

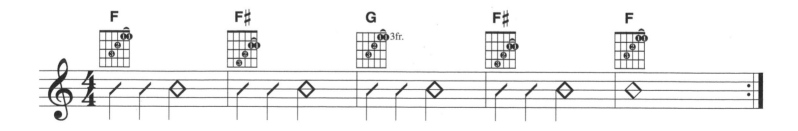

New Strum Pattern

45 Michael, Row the Boat Ashore

African American

Capo the 5th fret for singing. Key of F

continue strum pattern throughout

♩ = 104

1. Mi - chael, row the boat a - shore, Al - le - lu -
(2.) helped to trim the sail, Al - le - lu -
(3.) deep and the river is wide, Al - le - lu -

ia! Mi - chael, row the boat a - shore, Al - le -
ia! Sis - ter helped to trim the sail, Al - le -
ia! Green_____ pastures on the oth - er side, Al - le -

1. 2. etc.

lu - ia! 2. Sis - ter lu - ia!
lu - ia! 3. The river is

Last time

lu - ia!

Additional Lyrics

4. Jordan's river is chilly and cold, Alleluia!
   Chills the body but not the soul, Alleluia!

5. The river is deep and the river is wide, Alleluia!
   Milk and honey on the other side, Alleluia!

chord chops

The following chord progression works well as an introduction (intro) to a song in the key of Dm.

46 Dreamless Nights

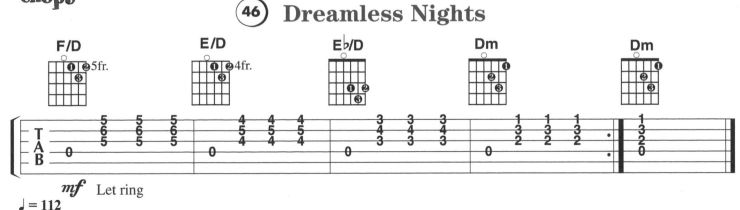

mf Let ring

♩ = 112

The use of a **tie** can help create a more interesting strum pattern. When two strums are tied, play the first strum only, allowing it to sound for the combined value of both strums.

Count: 1 - 2 - 3 - 4 - 1 - 2 - 3 4

New Strum Pattern

Count: 1 + 2 + (3) + 4 +

tie

(47) The Riddle Song

American Folksong

♩ = 96

1. I gave my love a cher - ry that

continue strum pattern throughout

has no stone; I gave my love a chick - en that

has no bone! I gave my love a sto - ry that has no

end, I gave my love a ba - by with no cry - ing.

Additional Lyrics

2. How can there be a cherry that has no stone?
And how can there be a chicken that has no bone?
And how can there be a story that has no end?
And how can there be a baby with no crying?

3. A cherry when it's blooming it has no stone,
A chicken when in the shell it has no bone.
The story of how I love you it has no end,
A baby when it's sleeping it's not crying.

The downstroke symbol in parentheses (⊓) indicates that your strumming hand goes through the motion of a downstroke without actually playing the strings. This technique keeps the down-up motion intact.

New Strum Pattern

(48) # Come Back, Liza

Capo the 5th fret for singing. Key of C

Jamaican Folksong

♩ = 104

1. Ev - 'ry time I 'mem - ber Li - za,

continue strum pattern throughout

wa - ter come — a me eye. Ev - 'ry time I think 'bout Li - za,

Chorus:

wa - ter come — a me eye. Come back, Li - za,

come back gal, — wa - ter come — a me eye. Come back Li - za,

come back gal, — wa - ter come — a me eye.

Additional Lyrics

2. I remember when love was new,
   Water come a me eye.
   There was one but now there's two,
   Water come a me eye.

3. In the shadow I stand awhile,
   Water come a me eye.
   Soon I'll see my Liza's smile,
   Water come a me eye.

music master

The ending used for *Come Back, Liza* is often referred to as the "cha-cha-cha" ending!

POWER CHORDS

Power chords are used in many popular and rock songs.

- They consist of only two notes: the **root** of the chord and the **fifth** of the chord.

- The unique sound of power chords makes them fun to play. They are often played on electric guitars using distortion.

- We will begin with the A5, D5, and E5 power chords, each using one left-hand finger as well as one open string. The root notes are in color.

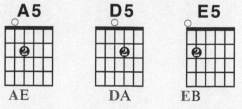

 The lowest-pitched note of power chords will almost always be the root. Power chords are usually played using only downstrokes. With practice, you will learn to play the two strings accurately (without striking other strings).

(49) Power Up!

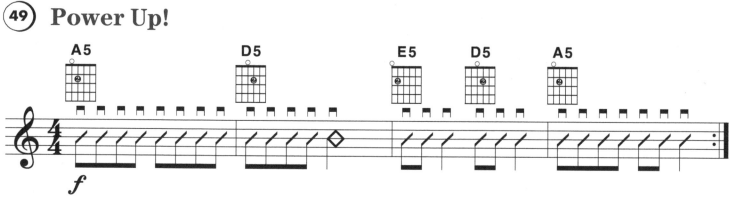

MOVABLE POWER CHORDS

Some power chords are **movable** because there are no open strings, such as G5.

- With this chord shape, your first finger will always play the root, and your third finger will always play the fifth.

- Keep the left-hand fingers spread out to make it easier to play this power chord shape.

- *Moving Around* uses an alternative version of the A5 chord. This fingering allows you to use guide fingers by playing all of the power chords on the sixth and fifth strings.

G5

(50) Moving Around

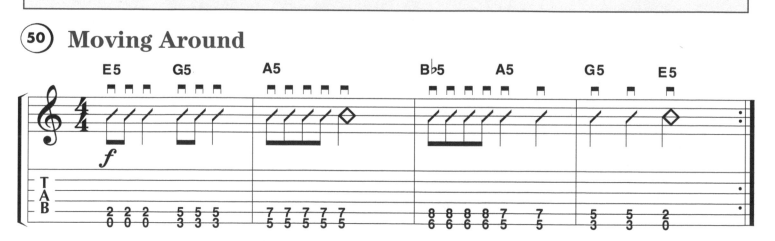

G1042

Power Chord Chart

51 Erie Canal

Thomas S. Allen

Capo the 5th fret for singing. Key of Dm

♩ = 104

1. I've got a mule, and her name is Sal,— fif - teen miles on the
   hauled some barg - es— in our day,— filled with lum - ber,—

E - rie Ca - nal. She's a good ol' work - er and a good ol' pal,—
coal— and hay. And— ev - 'ry inch of the— way I know, from

fif - teen miles on the E - rie Ca - nal. 2. We've
Al - ban - y to— Buf - fa - lo.

Additional Lyrics

3. We better get along
   on our way, old gal,
   fifteen miles on the Erie Canal.
   'Cause you bet your life
   I'd never part with Sal,
   fifteen miles on the Erie Canal.

4. Git up there, mule
   here comes a lock,
   We'll make Rome 'bout six o'clock.
   One more trip and back we'll go,
   right back home to Buffalo.

music master

This Erie Canal, completed in 1830, linked Buffalo to New York City. Towns along the way such as Albany, Buffalo, Rochester, Rome, and Syracuse prospered by using the canal. The canal boats were slow, but were responsible for carrying cargo and thousands of passengers.

Music of the past several hundred years has been mostly based on three **primary chords**. Although songs can use many chords, the primary chords are the most important. The primary chords are based on the first (I), fourth (IV), and the fifth (V) scale degrees of a given key. The V chord will usually be a seventh chord. See page 61 for more information on primary chords.

For example, here are the primary chords in the Key of E. The Key of E is often used in the blues, and therefore is a great starting point in learning blues chord progressions. Memorize the various names for each chord.

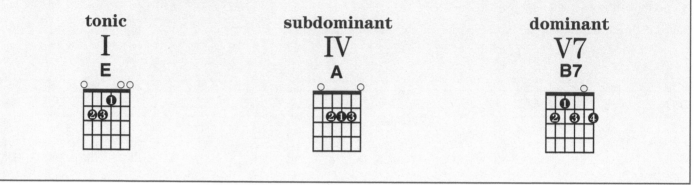

- **The 12-Bar Blues Progression** has been the basis for numerous pop, rock, and blues songs.
- This progression uses the primary chords (I, IV, and V7) from a given key.
- Using the Roman numerals as a guide, strum chords to *The 12-Bar Blues Progression* in the Key of E. You may use any strum pattern that you have learned.

⑤② The 12-Bar Blues Progression

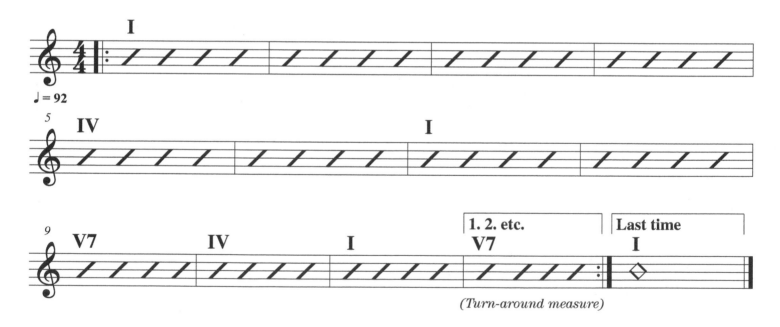

(Turn-around measure)

test
yourself

Can you strum chords to *The 12-Bar Blues Progression* in the Key of G? In the Key of C?

I	IV	V7
G	C	D7
C	F	G7

- *Rockin'* uses the **primary power chords** in the key of E, with some additional notes.
- This blues progression is only eight measures long, as opposed to the usual twelve measures.

(53) Rockin'

(Turn-around measure)

chord chops

Use the F chord shape (which is movable over all of the fingerboard) to play *Louie's Blues*. This piece uses the primary chords in the Key of F Major.

(54) Louie's Blues

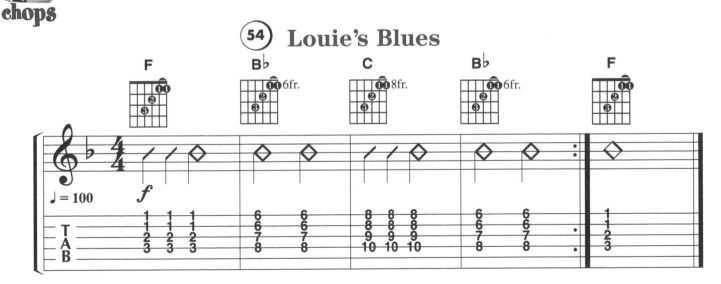

FINGERSTYLE (or FINGERPICKING)

- The right-hand thumb and fingers are often used to pluck the strings.

- Follow the right-hand position indicated in the photos very carefully. The proper position is very important in **fingerstyle** accompaniment.

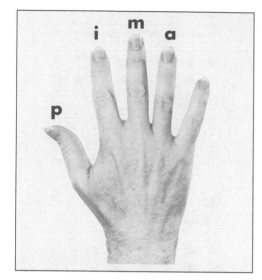

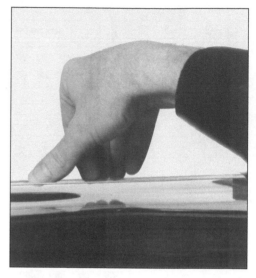

- Each finger has a letter name derived from the Spanish word.

  p = *pulgar* (thumb)
  i = *indice* (index)
  m = *media* (middle)
  a = *anular* (ring)

- Position your right hand toward the midpoint between the bridge and the fingerboard, or the edge of the soundhole.

- The wrist should be aligned naturally with the hand and forearm.

- The fingers (i, m, and a) should be held in a relaxed curve, as if you are holding a bubble.

- The thumb (p) is extended slightly, allowing the thumb and fingers to play without bumping into each other.

- The nails may be used to help produce a louder and more beautiful sound. File your nails so that they pass smoothly over the strings.

THE FREE STROKE

- Place (or prepare) the fingertip on the string. Play the string with a "scratching" motion, moving mostly from the knuckle.

- When playing free strokes, your finger will pass freely above the adjacent string (without touching it).

- Place (or prepare) the thumb on the string.

- Play the string with a forward and upward motion.

- Your thumb will pass freely above the adjacent string.

- Use free strokes when fingerpicking chords.

ARPEGGIOS AND BLOCK CHORDS

In an **arpeggio**, the notes of a chord are played one after another (instead of at the same time).
In a **block chord,** the notes of a chord are played together (at the same time).
Fingerstyle accompaniments often use arpeggios, block chords, or a combination of the two.

• When playing arpeggios, be sure to play very evenly, letting all of the notes ring out clearly.

(55) Silent Night

Words by Joseph Mohr
Music by Franz Gruber

Fingerstyle

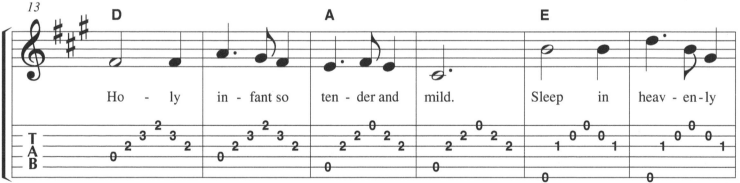

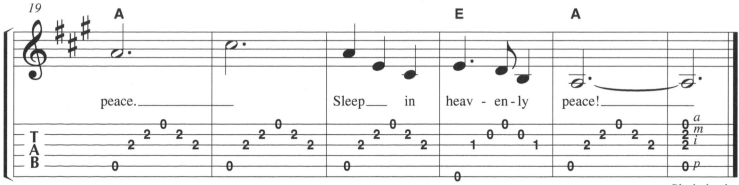

Block chord

SLASH CHORDS

A **slash chord** is a chord in which the lowest-pitched note is *not* the root. These chords are notated with two letters separated by a slash (see Em/D♯ in the song below). The first letter is the name of the chord. The second letter is the name of the bass note to be played.

Slash chords create interesting new sounds for chord accompaniments, and can provide a smooth transition between bass notes (lower-pitched notes) when changing from one chord to the next.

(56) It Makes Me Wonder

Fingerstyle

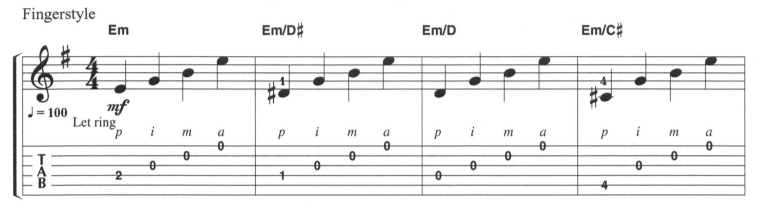

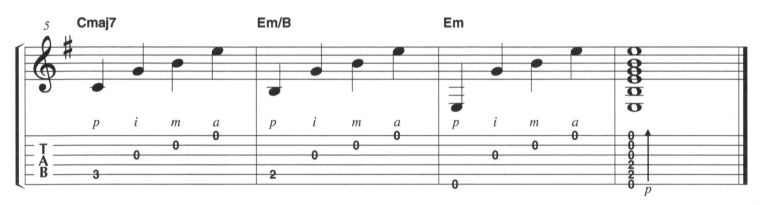

(57) Fingerpicking Good!

Fingerstyle

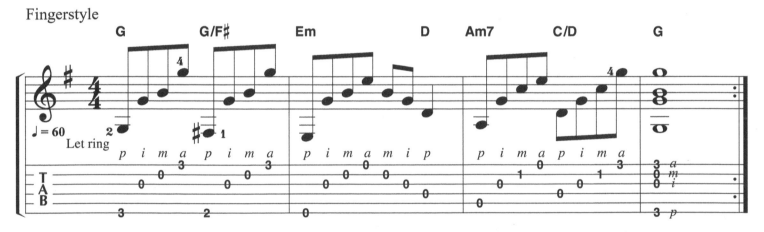

Popular songs may use many slash chords. It is not always necessary to include the bass note indicated, especially when playing along with other performers. With practice, you will become more comfortable playing slash chords.

50

(58) Take Me Out to the Ball Game

Words by Jack Norworth
Music by Albert von Tilzer

Capo the 5th fret for singing. Key of C

Here is a good solution for strumming the chords in measures 21-25.
Carefully observe the left-hand fingering.

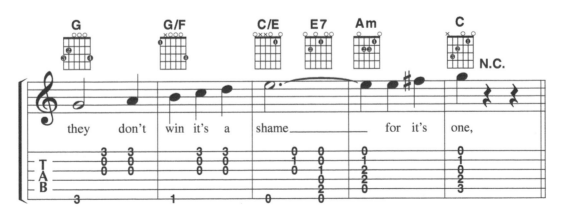

When Johnny Comes Marching Home Again

(59)

Louis Lambert

Capo the 2nd fret for singing. Key of F#m

♩ = 168

When John-ny comes march - ing home a - gain, Hur - rah!_____ Hur -

rah!_____ We'll give him a heart - y wel - come then, Hur -

rah!_____ Hur - rah!_____ The — men will cheer and the boys will

shout, the la - dies, they — will all turn out. And we'll all

feel grand when John-ny comes march - ing home._____

*You may also play fingerstyle block chords (as opposed to strumming)
on the song above. Try playing some of the earlier songs in this book using
fingerstyle techniques.*

This song dates back to the Civil War and is one of the few patriotic
songs written in a minor key. The lyrics, by Irish American bandleader
Patrick S. Gilmore, were published under the pen name of Louis Lambert.

⑥⓪ Auld Lang Syne

Words by Robert Burns
Scottish Melody

Capo the 2nd fret for singing. Key of E

Fingerstyle or Pickstyle

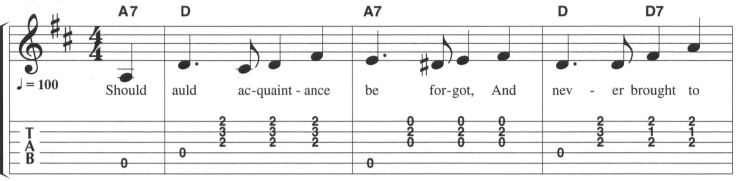

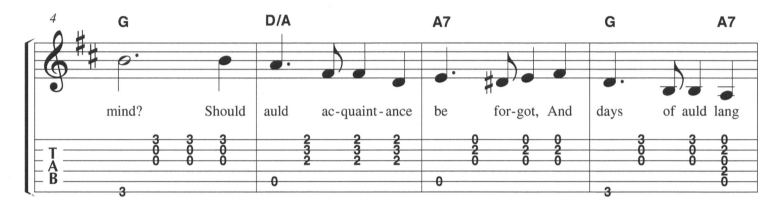

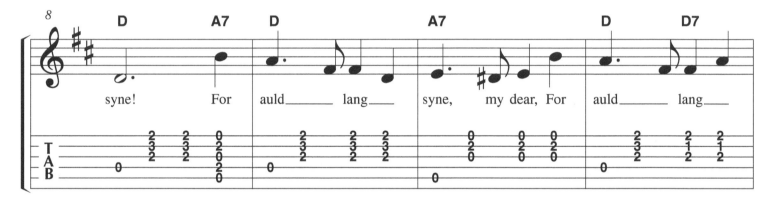

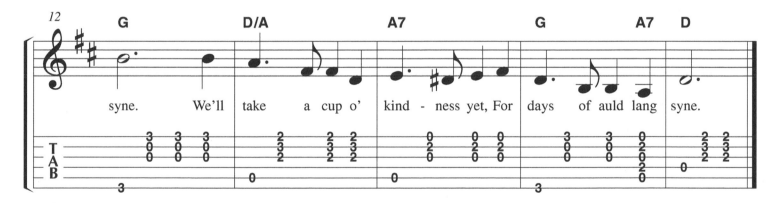

Auld Lang Syne has traditionally been played on New Year's Eve. Guy Lombardo and his "Royal Canadians" performed it annually on a radio show for many years. The title of this song of friendship is written in Scottish dialect, which translates to "Old Long Since."

(61) Morning Has Broken

Gaelic Melody

Morning Has Broken is based on a traditional Scottish Gaelic melody. It was popularized in 1971 when it was recorded by Cat Stevens. The familiar piano arrangement on Stevens' album was performed by Rick Wakeman, a classically trained keyboardist with the English progressive rock band *Yes*.

Rhythm Guitar Tips

Intro: *The easiest way to provide an introduction to a song is to strum the first chord for two or more measures.*

Ending: *Always play a pleasing, solid ending to any song. It can be abrupt, or a "let ring," but be sure that it makes a good ending for the song.*

⑥₂ Greensleeves
(What Child Is This)

English Folksong

continue the strum pattern

♩ = 104

continue the original strum pattern

ritard.

G1042

(63) Scarborough Fair

English Folksong

Capo the 5th fret for singing. Key of Dm

Additional Lyrics

2. Have her make me a cambric shirt.
   Parsley, sage, rosemary, and thyme.
   Without no seam nor fine needle work.
   And then she'll be a true love of mine.

3. Tell her to weave it in a sycamore wood lane.
   Parsley, sage, rosemary, and thyme.
   And gather it all with a basket of flowers.
   And then she'll be a true love of mine.

4. Have her wash it in yonder dry well.
   Parsley, sage, rosemary, and thyme.
   Where water ne'er sprung nor drop of rain fell.
   And then she'll be a true love of mine.

5. Dear, when thou has finished thy task.
   Parsley, sage, rosemary, and thyme.
   Come to me, my hand for to ask.
   For thou then art a true love of mine.

Scarborough was an important port in medieval England. Every autumn, a large fair with merchants and musicians was held at Scarborough. The lyrics relate the story of a young man who tells a hopeful young maiden that he will take her back only if she can complete certain impossible tasks.

G1042

The Star-Spangled Banner

Words by Francis Scott Key
Music by John Stafford Smith

Chords Used in This Book

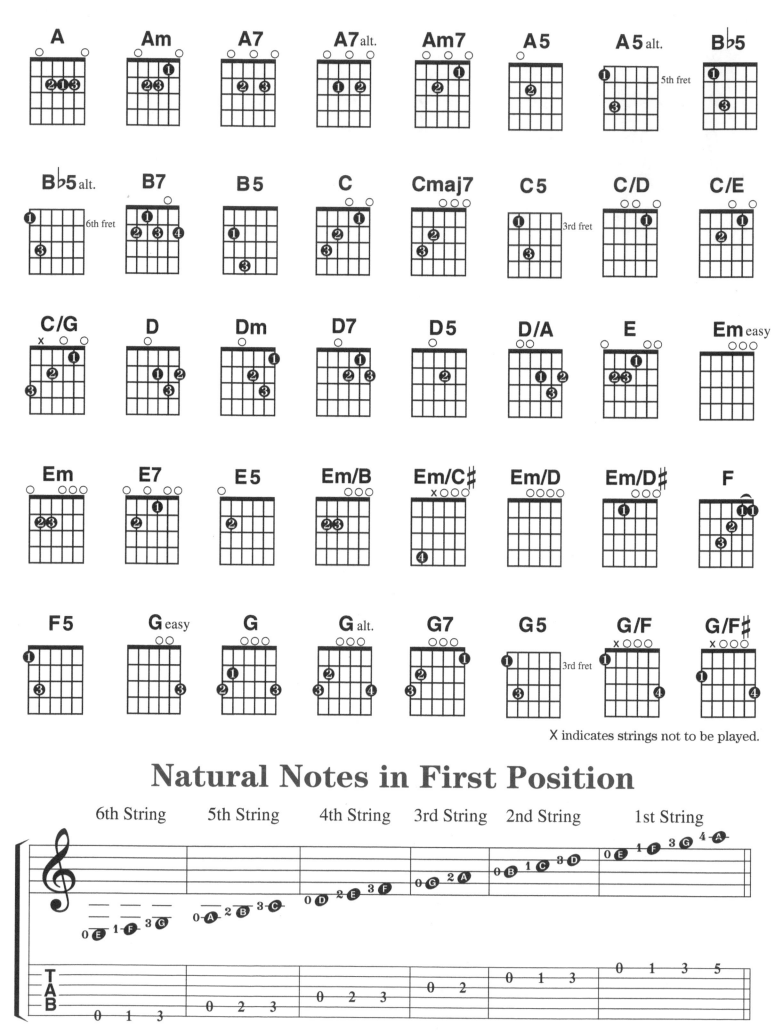

X indicates strings not to be played.

Natural Notes in First Position

G1042

Common Guitar Chords

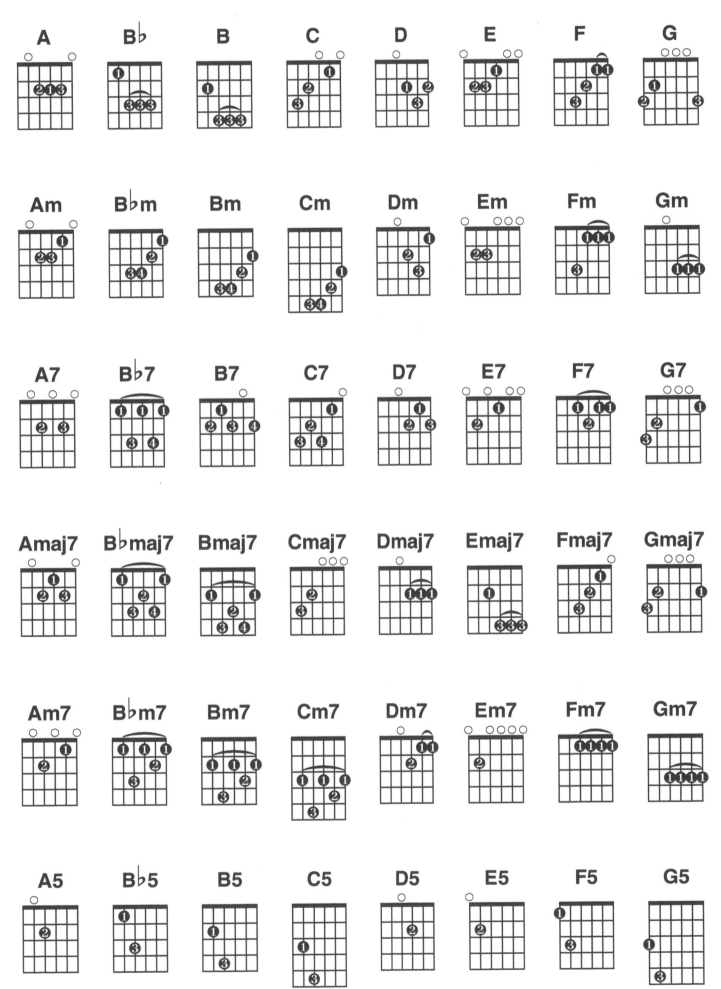

Strum and Fingerpicking Patterns

Pick Style

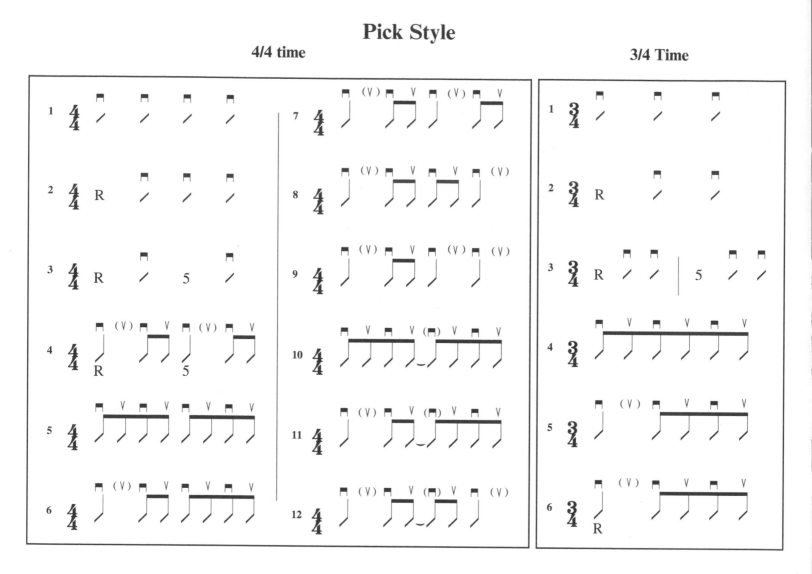

Fingerstyle

Primary Chords

The primary chords are based on the first (I), fourth (IV), and fifth (V) scale degrees of any given key. The chart below lists the primary chords used in "guitar friendly" keys.

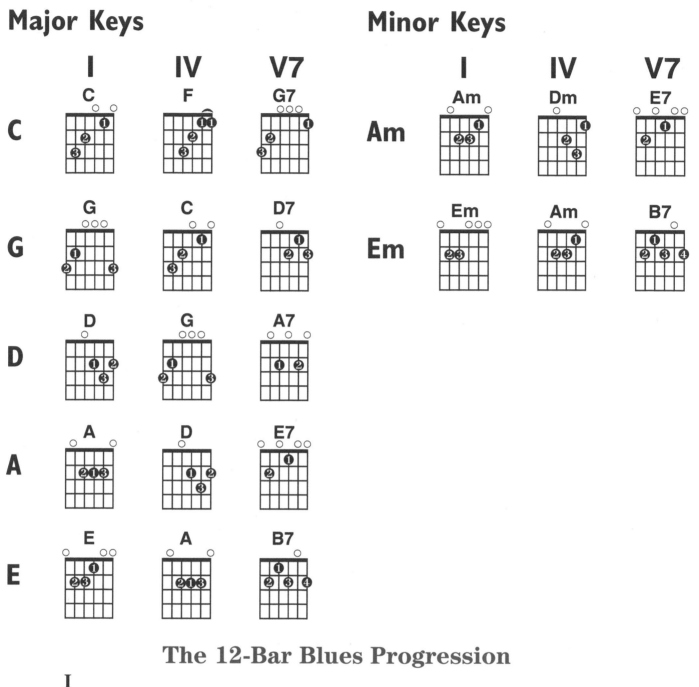

Major Keys

Minor Keys

The 12-Bar Blues Progression

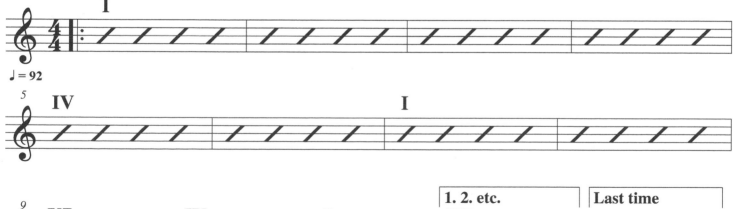

(Turn-around measure)

Movable Chords

Chords that use no open strings have a special feature. They may be moved up and down the fingerboard to form other chords. There are three common **movable chord** families on the guitar. The E, A, and C types of movable chords use the same *shapes* as the basic chords they are named after. By adding a **barre** (using one left-hand finger to play more than one string at a time), you can move the same shape up and down the fingerboard to make different chords.

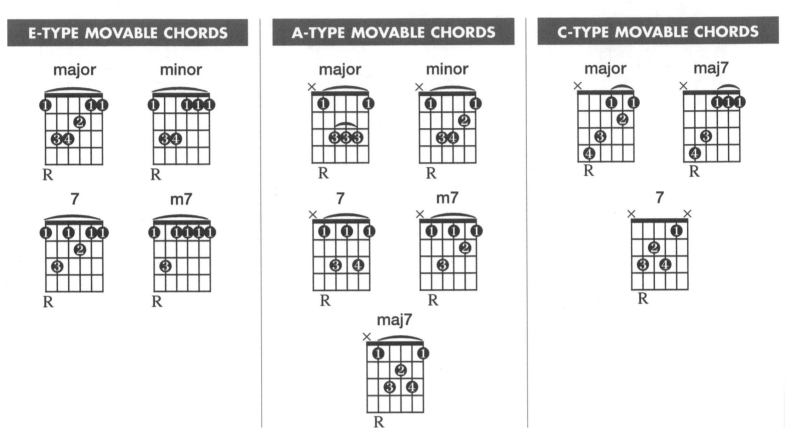

FIRST FINGER BARRE	E TYPE	A TYPE	C TYPE
Open (no barre)	E	A	C
1st Fret	F	A♯ (or B♭)	C♯ (or D♭)
2nd Fret	F♯ (or G♭)	B	D
3rd Fret	G	C	D♯ (or E♭)
4th Fret	G♯ (or A♭)	C♯ (or D♭)	E
5th Fret	A	D	F
6th Fret	A♯ (or B♭)	D♯ (or E♭)	F♯ (or G♭)
7th Fret	B	E	G
8th Fret	C	F	G♯ (or A♭)
9th Fret	C♯ (or D♭)	F♯ (or G♭)	A
10th Fret	D	G	A♯ (or B♭)
11th Fret	D♯ (or E♭)	G♯ (or A♭)	B
12th Fret	E	A	C
13th Fret	F	A♯ (or B♭)	C♯ (or D♭)

G1042

How to Use a Capo

A **capo** is a clamp that holds all six strings down on any given fret, raising the pitch of the open strings by one half step for every fret. For example, a capo placed on the first fret will make an E chord sound like an F, an A chord sound like a B♭, etc.

Using a Capo To Simplify a Difficult Key

A capo allows you to play comfortably in any key. For example, a song may be too hard to play in the key of E♭. One solution is to attach a capo on the third fret and play it as if it were in the key of C. You will, however, have to transpose every chord. Write the capoed chord name above the original chord, using the chart below. Your teacher will help you.

Using a Capo To Play in Different Keys

A capo may be used to change the key of a song for a more comfortable singing range. The following chart will help you play in common "guitar" keys while the guitar *sounds* in another.

CAPO THIS FRET ↓	PLAY IN THESE "GUITAR" KEYS				
	A	C	D	E	G
	CAPOED GUITAR SOUNDS IN THESE KEYS				
1	B♭ (or A♯)	D♭ (or C♯)	E♭ (or D♯)	F	A♭ (or G♯)
2	B	D	E	G♭ (or F♯)	A
3	C	E♭ (or D♯)	F	G	B♭ (or A♯)
4	D♭ (or C♯)	E	G♭ (or F♯)	A♭ (or G♯)	B
5	D	F	G	A	C
6	E♭ (or D♯)	G♭ (or F♯)	A♭ (or G♯)	B♭ (or A♯)	D♭ (or C♯)
7	E	G	A	B	D
8	F	A♭ (or G♯)	B♭ (or A♯)	C	E♭ (or D♯)
9	G♭ (or F♯)	A	B	D♭ (or C♯)	E
10	G	B♭ (or A♯)	C	D	F
11	A♭ (or G♯)	B	D♭ (or C♯)	E♭ (or D♯)	G♭ (or F♯)

Glossary

SIGN	TERM	DEFINITION
	Chorus:	A section of a song that is repeated after each verse. (pg. 17)
⊓	**downstroke**	Strumming the strings with a downward movement. (pg. 4, 7, 8)
p mf f	**dynamics**	Symbols or words which indicate softness or loudness. *p* (*piano*) soft; *mf* (*mezzo forte*) medium loud; *f* (*forte*) loud. (pg. 15)
⌢	*fermata*	Indicates that a note or rest should be held longer than usual. (pg. 18)
	1st and 2nd endings	After playing music in the 1st ending bracket, repeat and then play the music in the 2nd ending bracket (in place of the 1st). (pg. 27)
♭	**flat**	Lowers the pitch of a note by one fret (one half step). (pg. 22)
	Let ring	Allow the strings to vibrate as long as possible. (pg. 26)
	lyrics	Words to a song that are sung with the melody. (pg. 7)
♩ = 60	**metronome mark**	Indicates the number of beats per minute. (pg. 8)
♮	**natural**	Cancels a sharp or flat used earlier. (pg. 26)
N.C.	**No Chord**	No chords are to be played. Dampen (stop from vibrating) the strings with your right or left hand. (pg. 26)
1 2 3 4 ① ② ③ ④ ⑤ ⑥	**numbers**	2 indicates to use the second finger of the left hand; ② indicates to play on the second string. (pg. 4, 5, 7)
	pick-up notes	One or more notes that are played before the first complete measure of music. (pg. 12)
:‖	**repeat sign**	Play a section of music again after seeing this sign. (pg. 8)
▬ ▬ ╕	**rest**	Indicates a moment of silence in music. (pg. 6, 20)
	ritard.	Gradually becoming slower. (pg. 55)
	root note	The letter name of the chord. Use the lowest-pitched root when strumming chords. (pg. 28)
♯	**sharp**	Raises the pitch of a note by one fret (one half step). (pg. 8)
G/B	**slash chord**	A chord in which the lowest-pitched note is not the root. G/B is a G chord with a B as the lowest-pitched note. (pg. 50)
♩♩	**tie**	A curved line connecting two strums (or notes). Play the first strum only, allowing it to sound for the combined value of both tied strums. (pg. 42)
∨	**upstroke**	Strumming the strings with an upward movement. (pg. 4, 26, 32)
	Verse:	Lyrics that change throughout the song. (pg. 17)
C/G		The X symbol over a string in a fingerboard diagram indicates that the string is not to be played. Either do not play the string with your right hand or mute (dampen) the string with your left hand. (pg. 58)

G1042